A Modern Minimalist Journal for Baby's First Year

LeAnna Weller Smith

LOWERCASE INK
NEW YORK

lovingly made for

_____

born on

| MONTH | DAY | YEAR |

_____
TIME

_____
WEIGHT

_____
LENGTH

about this journal

This journal is a place to jot down those little moments that happen during the whirlwind that is parenthood—the funny times, the challenges, and the small things your baby does that you never want to forget. From family details, through baby's first year in a month by month format, there is space to record the ways in which your baby is growing and changing and also to reflect on the little moments that have meant something to you.

Tuck this journal in a pocket or diaper bag, so you can take it out and quickly jot down a memory before it slips away. Or, you can pick it up during a quiet moment and write down what you remember from recent days or months. In the end, you'll have a wonderful family keepsake. Your child will be able to see what you were thinking and feeling as you watched them grow.

enjoy every moment

								RELATIONSHIP
MONTH		DAY		YEAR			

*attach a
favorite picture*

FULL NAME: _____

BIRTHDAY: _____

PARENTS' NAMES: _____

_____

SIBLINGS' NAMES: _____

_____

_____

the family
you are a part of

HOMETOWN: _____

EDUCATION: _____

CURRENT JOB: _____

RELIGION/SPIRITUALITY: _____

HOBBIES: _____

_____

_____

FAVORITE SONG: _____

FAVORITE MOVIE: _____

FAVORITE MEAL: _____

FAVORITE MEMORY FROM CHILDHOOD: _____

_____

_____

_____

FAVORITE MEMORY FROM ADULTHOOD: _____

_____

_____

_____

_____

| MONTH | DAY | YEAR |

RELATIONSHIP

attach a favorite picture

FULL NAME: _____

BIRTHDAY: _____

PARENTS' NAMES: _____

_____

SIBLINGS' NAMES: _____

_____

_____

the family
you are a part of

HOMETOWN: _____

EDUCATION: _____

CURRENT JOB: _____

RELIGION/SPIRITUALITY: _____

HOBBIES: _____

_____

_____

FAVORITE SONG: _____

FAVORITE MOVIE: _____

FAVORITE MEAL: _____

FAVORITE MEMORY FROM CHILDHOOD: _____

_____

_____

_____

FAVORITE MEMORY FROM ADULTHOOD: _____

_____

_____

_____

_____

Collage wedding photos, pictures of your home, family pet, favorite things, etc.

the family
before you were born

HOW WE MET:

DATE OF WEDDING OR UNION:

WHAT THAT DAY WAS LIKE:

WHERE WE LIVE NOW:

WE FOUND OUT WE WERE PREGNANT ON:

FAVORITE MOMENTS FROM PREGNANCY:

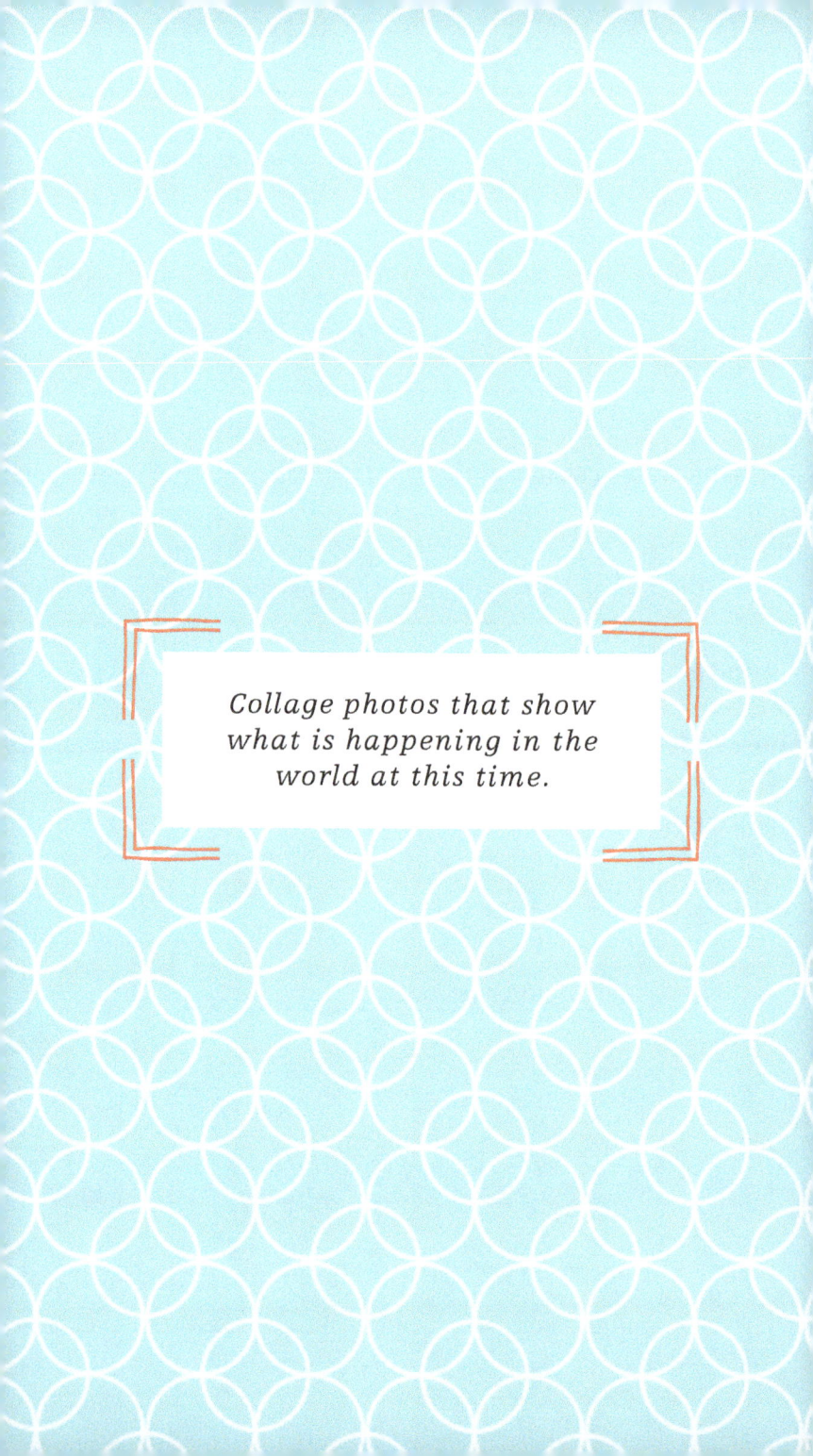

the world
when you were born

ON THE RADIO/FAVORITE BANDS

AT THE MOVIES/ON TV

IN THE NEWS

FASHION/TRENDS

LATEST GADGETS

TIDBITS

favorite social media: _____

MONTH	DAY	YEAR	PICTURE TAKEN HERE

attach a favorite picture

BIRTHDAY STATS

DATE		EYE COLOR	
TIME		HAIR/NO HAIR	
SEX		HAIR COLOR	
WEIGHT		BIRTH MARKS	
LENGTH		LOOKS LIKE	

all about you
the day you were born

FULL NAME: _____

NICKNAME: _____

WHY WE PICKED THIS NAME: _____

_____

_____

HOSPITAL NAME: _____

TYPE OF BIRTH: _____

LABOR LASTED: _____

PEOPLE PRESENT DURING YOUR BIRTH: _____

_____

_____

_____

_____

MOST MEMORABLE MOMENTS FROM YOUR BIRTH: _____

_____

_____

_____

_____

lottery numbers for the day: _____

MONTH DAY   YEAR   PICTURE TAKEN HERE

attach a favorite picture

FAVORITE MOMENTS FROM YOUR FIRST FEW DAYS AT HOME:

LENGTH		
WEIGHT		
MILESTONES		

the first few days
with you at home

YOU CAME HOME ON: _____

PEOPLE WHO VISITED OR HELPED TAKE CARE OF YOU: _____

_____

_____

FIRST PERSON TO CHANGE YOUR DIAPER: _____

_____

WHEN YOU CRIED, WE SOOTHED YOU BY: _____

_____

_____

_____

YOU TOOK YOUR FIRST BATH ON: _____

THE DAY WE FOUND OUT IF YOU WERE AN INNIE OR AN OUTTIE: _____

YOU TOOK YOUR FIRST OUTING TO: _____

_____

HOW WE FELT DURING YOUR FIRST FEW DAYS HOME: _____

_____

_____

_____

_____

MONTH DAY YEAR

sonogram

MEMORIES/EMOTIONS FROM THIS DAY

birth day

MONTH   DAY   YEAR

MEASUREMENTS   FAVORITE MOMENTS

LENGTH	
WEIGHT	

1 month

MONTH   DAY   YEAR

PHOTO OPP.

Each month, take a photo of baby in the same spot with a small but legible sign on or near them that states their age. Attach the photos into this journal as a fun way to see baby's growth over the first year.

MEASUREMENTS   FAVORITE MOMENTS

LENGTH	
WEIGHT	

MONTH DAY YEAR

2 months

MEASUREMENTS FAVORITE MOMENTS

LENGTH	
WEIGHT	

MONTH   DAY   YEAR

3 months

MEASUREMENTS   FAVORITE MOMENTS

LENGTH	
WEIGHT	

MONTH DAY YEAR

4 months

MEASUREMENTS FAVORITE MOMENTS

LENGTH	
WEIGHT	

MONTH DAY YEAR

5 months

MEASUREMENTS   FAVORITE MOMENTS

LENGTH	
WEIGHT	

MONTH   DAY   YEAR

6 months

MEASUREMENTS   FAVORITE MOMENTS

LENGTH	
WEIGHT	

MONTH DAY YEAR

MEASUREMENTS   FAVORITE MOMENTS

LENGTH	
WEIGHT	

MONTH   DAY   YEAR

8 months

MEASUREMENTS   FAVORITE MOMENTS

LENGTH	
WEIGHT	

MONTH DAY YEAR

9 month

MEASUREMENTS   FAVORITE MOMENTS

LENGTH	
WEIGHT	

MONTH DAY YEAR

10 months

MEASUREMENTS FAVORITE MOMENTS

LENGTH	
WEIGHT	

11 month

MONTH DAY YEAR

MEASUREMENTS   FAVORITE MOMENTS

LENGTH	
WEIGHT	

MONTH　DAY　YEAR

12 months

MEASUREMENTS　FAVORITE MOMENTS

LENGTH	
WEIGHT	

year

ONE

in words

Collage favorite photos or other memorabilia from this time.

the first month
how you've changed

THINGS YOU'VE LEARNED TO DO:

HOW YOU HAVE CHANGED:

YOUR SCHEDULE IS:

MONTH   DAY   YEAR   PICTURE TAKEN HERE

attach a favorite picture

MEASUREMENTS:

LENGTH		WEIGHT	

FAVORITE MOMENTS:

my favorite song to sing to you is: _____

the first month
how you've changed

THINGS YOU LIKE TO DO:

THING YOU DON'T LIKE TO DO:

SOME OF THE CUTEST THINGS YOU DO:

THINGS WE'VE LEARNED ABOUT PARENTING:

SPECIAL MOMENTS WITH YOU:

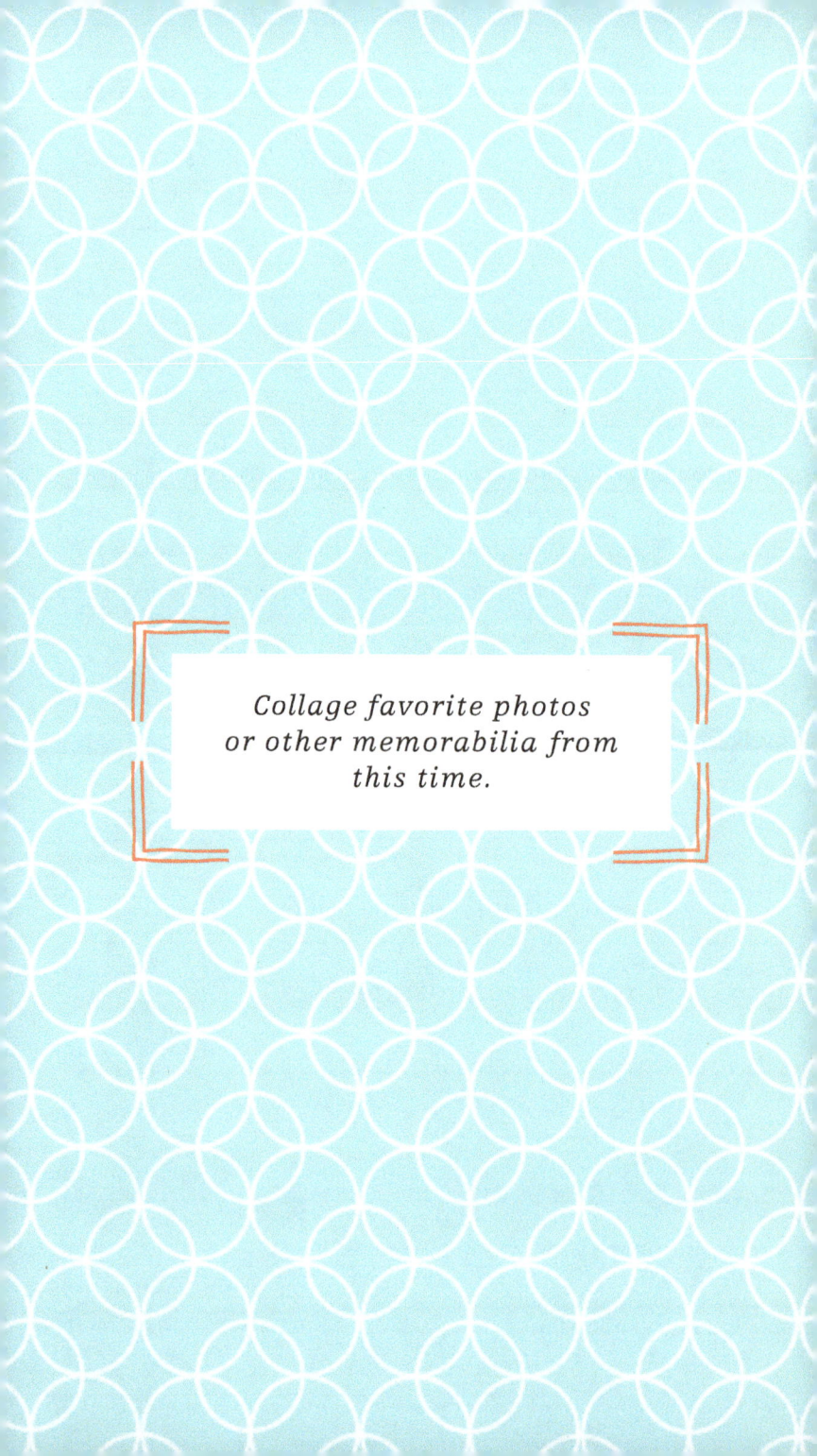
Collage favorite photos or other memorabilia from this time.

the second month
how you've changed

THINGS YOU'VE LEARNED TO DO:

HOW YOU HAVE CHANGED:

YOUR SCHEDULE IS:

MONTH	DAY	YEAR

PICTURE TAKEN HERE

attach a favorite picture

MEASUREMENTS:

LENGTH		WEIGHT	

FAVORITE MOMENTS:

my favorite song to sing to you is: _____

the second month
how you've changed

THINGS YOU LIKE TO DO:

THING YOU DON'T LIKE TO DO:

SOME OF THE CUTEST THINGS YOU DO:

THINGS WE'VE LEARNED ABOUT PARENTING:

SPECIAL MOMENTS WITH YOU:

Collage favorite photos or other memorabilia from this time.

the third month
how you've changed

THINGS YOU'VE LEARNED TO DO:

HOW YOU HAVE CHANGED:

YOUR SCHEDULE IS:

MONTH   DAY   YEAR   PICTURE TAKEN HERE

*attach a
favorite picture*

MEASUREMENTS:

LENGTH		WEIGHT	

FAVORITE MOMENTS:

my favorite song to sing to you is: _____

the third month
how you've changed

THINGS YOU LIKE TO DO:

THING YOU DON'T LIKE TO DO:

SOME OF THE CUTEST THINGS YOU DO:

THINGS WE'VE LEARNED ABOUT PARENTING:

SPECIAL MOMENTS WITH YOU:

Collage favorite photos or other memorabilia from this time.

the fourth month
how you've changed

THINGS YOU'VE LEARNED TO DO:

HOW YOU HAVE CHANGED:

YOUR SCHEDULE IS:

MONTH	DAY	YEAR

PICTURE TAKEN HERE

attach a favorite picture

MEASUREMENTS:

LENGTH		WEIGHT	

FAVORITE MOMENTS:

my favorite song to sing to you is: _____

the fourth month
how you've changed

THINGS YOU LIKE TO DO:

THING YOU DON'T LIKE TO DO:

SOME OF THE CUTEST THINGS YOU DO:

THINGS WE'VE LEARNED ABOUT PARENTING:

SPECIAL MOMENTS WITH YOU:

Collage favorite photos or other memorabilia from this time.

the fifth month
how you've changed

THINGS YOU'VE LEARNED TO DO:

HOW YOU HAVE CHANGED:

YOUR SCHEDULE IS:

| MONTH | DAY | YEAR |

PICTURE TAKEN HERE

attach a favorite picture

MEASUREMENTS:

LENGTH		WEIGHT	

FAVORITE MOMENTS:

my favorite song to sing to you is: _____

the fifth month
how you've changed

THINGS YOU LIKE TO DO:

THING YOU DON'T LIKE TO DO:

SOME OF THE CUTEST THINGS YOU DO:

THINGS WE'VE LEARNED ABOUT PARENTING:

SPECIAL MOMENTS WITH YOU:

Collage favorite photos or other memorabilia from this time.

the sixth month
how you've changed

THINGS YOU'VE LEARNED TO DO:

HOW YOU HAVE CHANGED:

YOUR SCHEDULE IS:

MONTH	DAY	YEAR

PICTURE TAKEN HERE

attach a favorite picture

MEASUREMENTS:

LENGTH		WEIGHT	

FAVORITE MOMENTS:

my favorite song to sing to you is: _____

the sixth month
how you've changed

THINGS YOU LIKE TO DO:

THING YOU DON'T LIKE TO DO:

SOME OF THE CUTEST THINGS YOU DO:

THINGS WE'VE LEARNED ABOUT PARENTING:

SPECIAL MOMENTS WITH YOU:

Collage favorite photos or other memorabilia from this time.

the seventh month
how you've changed

THINGS YOU'VE LEARNED TO DO:

HOW YOU HAVE CHANGED:

YOUR SCHEDULE IS:

MONTH	DAY	YEAR

PICTURE TAKEN HERE

attach a favorite picture

MEASUREMENTS:

LENGTH		WEIGHT	

FAVORITE MOMENTS:

my favorite song to sing to you is: _____

the seventh month
how you've changed

THINGS YOU LIKE TO DO:

THING YOU DON'T LIKE TO DO:

SOME OF THE CUTEST THINGS YOU DO:

THINGS WE'VE LEARNED ABOUT PARENTING:

SPECIAL MOMENTS WITH YOU:

Collage favorite photos or other memorabilia from this time.

the eighth month
how you've changed

THINGS YOU'VE LEARNED TO DO:

HOW YOU HAVE CHANGED:

YOUR SCHEDULE IS:

MONTH DAY YEAR

PICTURE TAKEN HERE

attach a favorite picture

MEASUREMENTS:

LENGTH		WEIGHT	

FAVORITE MOMENTS:

my favorite song to sing to you is: _____

the eighth month
how you've changed

THINGS YOU LIKE TO DO:

THING YOU DON'T LIKE TO DO:

SOME OF THE CUTEST THINGS YOU DO:

THINGS WE'VE LEARNED ABOUT PARENTING:

SPECIAL MOMENTS WITH YOU:

Collage favorite photos or other memorabilia from this time.

the nineth month
how you've changed

THINGS YOU'VE LEARNED TO DO:

HOW YOU HAVE CHANGED:

YOUR SCHEDULE IS:

MONTH　DAY　YEAR

PICTURE TAKEN HERE

attach a favorite picture

MEASUREMENTS:

LENGTH		WEIGHT	

FAVORITE MOMENTS:

my favorite song to sing to you is: _____

the nineth month
how you've changed

THINGS YOU LIKE TO DO:

THING YOU DON'T LIKE TO DO:

SOME OF THE CUTEST THINGS YOU DO:

THINGS WE'VE LEARNED ABOUT PARENTING:

SPECIAL MOMENTS WITH YOU:

Collage favorite photos or other memorabilia from this time.

the tenth month
how you've changed

THINGS YOU'VE LEARNED TO DO:

HOW YOU HAVE CHANGED:

YOUR SCHEDULE IS:

MONTH DAY YEAR PICTURE TAKEN HERE

attach a favorite picture

MEASUREMENTS:

LENGTH		WEIGHT	

FAVORITE MOMENTS:

my favorite song to sing to you is: _____

the tenth month
how you've changed

THINGS YOU LIKE TO DO:

THING YOU DON'T LIKE TO DO:

SOME OF THE CUTEST THINGS YOU DO:

THINGS WE'VE LEARNED ABOUT PARENTING:

SPECIAL MOMENTS WITH YOU:

Collage favorite photos or other memorabilia from this time.

the eleventh month
how you've changed

THINGS YOU'VE LEARNED TO DO:

HOW YOU HAVE CHANGED:

YOUR SCHEDULE IS:

MONTH DAY YEAR   PICTURE TAKEN HERE

attach a favorite picture

MEASUREMENTS:

LENGTH		WEIGHT	

FAVORITE MOMENTS:

my favorite song to sing to you is: _____

the eleventh month
how you've changed

THINGS YOU LIKE TO DO:

THING YOU DON'T LIKE TO DO:

SOME OF THE CUTEST THINGS YOU DO:

THINGS WE'VE LEARNED ABOUT PARENTING:

SPECIAL MOMENTS WITH YOU:

Collage favorite photos or other memorabilia from this time.

the twelfth month
how you've changed

THINGS YOU'VE LEARNED TO DO:

HOW YOU HAVE CHANGED:

YOUR SCHEDULE IS:

MONTH		DAY		YEAR			

PICTURE TAKEN HERE

attach a favorite picture

MEASUREMENTS:

LENGTH		WEIGHT	

FAVORITE MOMENTS:

my favorite song to sing to you is: _____

the twelfth month
how you've changed

THINGS YOU LIKE TO DO:

THING YOU DON'T LIKE TO DO:

SOME OF THE CUTEST THINGS YOU DO:

THINGS WE'VE LEARNED ABOUT PARENTING:

SPECIAL MOMENTS WITH YOU:

Photo of the birthday baby!

Birthday Celebration
how we celebrated

DATE OF OUR CELEBRATION:

PARTY THEME:

CAKE OR NO CAKE:

WHO WAS INVITED:

FAVORITE MEMORIES

MONTH   DAY   YEAR   PICTURE TAKEN HERE

*attach
favorite party
pictures*

*attach
favorite party
pictures*

special deliveries
things you received

DATE RECEIVED	FROM	DESCRIPTION

special deliveries
things you received

DATE RECEIVED	FROM	DESCRIPTION

take a pic of baby in their new gift to send in the thank you card.

special deliveries
things you received

DATE RECEIVED	FROM	DESCRIPTION

special deliveries
things you received

DATE RECEIVED	FROM	DESCRIPTION

take a pic of baby playing with their new gift and email it as a thank you!

special deliveries
things you received

DATE RECEIVED	FROM	DESCRIPTION

special deliveries
things you received

DATE RECEIVED	FROM	DESCRIPTION

take a pic of baby and their new gift to send in the thank you card.

special deliveries
things you received

DATE RECEIVED	FROM	DESCRIPTION

special deliveries
things you received

DATE RECEIVED	FROM	DESCRIPTION

take a video of baby playing with their new gift and email it to say thank you!

special deliveries
things you received

DATE RECEIVED	FROM	DESCRIPTION

special deliveries
things you received

DATE RECEIVED	FROM	DESCRIPTION

next time you visit, have baby wearing their gift to show how cute it is.

special deliveries
things you received

DATE RECEIVED	FROM	DESCRIPTION

special deliveries
things you received

DATE RECEIVED	FROM	DESCRIPTION

take a pic of baby and their gift with the person and send it as a thank you.

special deliveries
things you received

DATE RECEIVED	FROM	DESCRIPTION

special deliveries
things you received

DATE RECEIVED	FROM	DESCRIPTION

take a pic of baby's new gift in their room to send in the thank you card.

All parts of this journal is copyrighted by
LeAnna Weller Smith

Unauthorized use, duplication, and/or distribution of
this material without express and written permission from
LeAnna Weller Smith is strictly prohibited.

First Printing © 2020 LeAnna Weller Smith

Hardcover: ISBN: 978-1-7342760-0-8
Paperback: ISBN: 978-1-7342760-1-5

Design: Weller Smith Design, LLC
www.wellersmithdesign.com

Published by: Lowercase Ink
www.lowercaseink.com

**Visit www.lowercaseink.com/welcomelittleone for
companion products and more information.**